I am a

JIGSAW

BLOOMSBURY EDUCATION
Bloomsbury Publishing Plc
50 Bedford Square, London, WC1B 3DP, UK

BLOOMSBURY, BLOOMSBURY EDUCATION and the Diana logo are
trademarks of Bloomsbury Publishing Plc

First published in 2019 by Bloomsbury Publishing Plc
Text and collection copyright © Roger Stevens, 2019
Illustrations copyright © Spike Gerrell, 2019

Roger Stevens and Spike Gerrell have asserted their rights under the Copyright,
Designs and Patents Act, 1988, to be identified as Author and Illustrator of this work

A catalogue record for this book is available from the British Library

ISBN: PB: 978-1-4729-5819-8; ePDF: 978-1-4729-5817-4; ePub: 978-1-4729-5816-7

2 4 6 8 10 9 7 5 3 1

Text design by Cathy Tincknell

Printed and bound in by CPI Group (UK) Ltd, Croydon, CR0 4YY

MIX
Paper from
responsible sources
FSC® C020471

All papers used by Bloomsbury Publishing Plc are natural, recyclable products from
wood grown in well managed forests. The manufacturing processes conform to the
environmental regulations of the country of origin

To find out more about our authors and books visit www.bloomsbury.com and sign
up for our newsletters

ROGER STEVENS

I am a JIGSAW

Illustrated by
SPIKE GERRELL

BLOOMSBURY EDUCATION
LONDON OXFORD NEW YORK NEW DELHI SYDNEY

CONTENTS

PART TWO: HOW TO WRITE PUZZLE POEMS

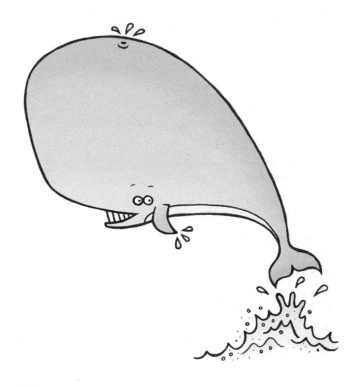

INTRODUCTION

Welcome to *I am a Jigsaw*, a book full of puzzling poems and words that would rather play hide-and-seek than be sensible and sit in a chair to be read quietly.

Poetry that uses riddles and puzzles is not new. The first riddle that we know about comes from a story from Ancient Greece, written more than 2,500 years ago. It tells the tale of Oedipus, the hero who prevented the destruction of Thebes. He managed to answer a seemingly unsolvable puzzle asked by the Sphinx, a creature with the head of a woman, the body of a lion and the wings of a bird. (There were some very strange animals around in those days!) The Sphinx asked: 'What walks on four legs in the morning, two legs in the afternoon and three legs in the evening?'

Another very old riddle was found on a stone tablet from the site of the city of Ur, dating from the sixteenth century BCE. It asked: 'A House. You enter it blind. You leave being able to see.' Do you know what it is? If you don't, you'll find the answer to both this and the riddle of the Sphinx at the bottom of the page opposite.

Riddles were a popular form of entertainment for ancient kings and their courts. The Greeks and Romans loved them. And the Egyptians were always up for a good picture puzzle, sometimes known as a rebus. Riddles and puzzles were popular well before modern printing was invented and many were passed on by word of mouth.

Riddles abound in children's nursery rhymes, but also in great works such as Beowulf, which was first written down around 1,000 years ago and is thought to be the oldest surviving poem in Old English. They were well loved through the Middle Ages and never really went out of fashion, so they are still popular today.

In this book, I've collected together as many different kinds of riddles and puzzles as I could. Some are traditional, the original writers long forgotten, but most of them have been written by those I consider to be among the best children's poets around today. And I have been interested in riddles as long as I can remember, so you might notice that many of the poems have been written by me.

A school

Man. We begin our life crawling on our hands and knees. Then we walk erect. Finally, in very old age we use the aid of a cane to walk.

PART ONE
RIDDLES IN RHYME

The first three sections of the book contain lots of different kinds of puzzle poems. We start with quite easy riddles, to give you a nice gentle introduction to it, but you will notice they get more difficult as you work through them. Then we will go on to look at some specific types of puzzle poems – I'll tell you a little more about those when we get there.

You'll find the answers to each riddle at the bottom of the page.

Good luck and happy puzzling!

1

Easy Peasy

Second-Hand Poem

You rarely have enough of me. I never, ever sleep.
Try and save me if you like – but sadly, I won't keep.
People often waste me, but they'll miss me
    when I'm gone –
you see, I wait for no one. I am always marching on.

Laura Mucha

Time

Around Riddle

You'll find me in space as you approach Jupiter
I am no easy riddle
I surround cities with trees and fields of green
And sometimes I circle your middle

Roger Stevens

A belt

Splash!

No matter how I try
to keep them warm and dry,
my feet (I don't know why)
refuse to pass one by,
and they insist that I
go wading through the sky.

Carol Samuelson-Woodson

Puddles

Under the Bridge

If you clap, I'll CLAP, clap, clap.
If you snap, I'll SNAP, snap, snap.
If you yell, I'll YELL, yell, yell.
Have a secret?
I'll TELL, tell, tell.

Suzy Levinson

An echo

A Place to Puzzle

Its façade is well known as exquisite,
It's a place that all tourists should visit,
The flagpole is bare
When the Queen isn't there,
It's in need of repair, but what is it?

Annie Fisher

Buckingham Palace

An Unusual Pet

With a wheel instead of a tail,
It fits neatly into your hand,
Allows you to click on your mail
And follows your every command.

Tracey Blance

A mouse

Hello

You saw me where I never was
and where I could not be.
And yet within that very place,
my face you often see. What am I?

Anon

A reflection

An Unexpected Riddle

I suddenly explode
Sending moisture everywhere
And as I disappear
Someone often says a prayer

Roger Stevens

A sneeze

9

Three Brothers

Three brothers share a family sport: a non-stop
    marathon
The oldest one is fat and short and trudges slowly on
The middle brother's tall and slim and keeps a
    steady pace
The youngest runs just like the wind, a-speeding
    through the race
'He's young in years, we let him run,' the other
    brothers say,
''Cause though he's surely number one,
    he's second, in a way.'

Anon

*The hands on a clock
(hour, minute, second)*

Tricky Teasers

On a Roll

A riddle am I, a cool paradiddle
I am thunderously slow, or as fast as a fiddle
In a band my best friend is the bass guitar
Bom badah bombadah bombadah dah

Roger Stevens

Drums (a paradiddle is a drum roll)

Not a Cow

Though not a cow
I have horns
Though not an ass
I carry a pack-saddle
And wherever I go
I leave silver behind me

Anon

A snail

Aye Aye

I make things bigger,
Sharper and clearer
My sister does distance
My brother does nearer
I can help when it's sunny
I can improve your health
But I wouldn't like to draw
Attention to myself

Roger Stevens

Spectacles

Find Me

The first hides in mystery,
the moon and amaze

the second in charm,
enchanting and daze

the third helps make dragons,
bewitching and genie

the fourth's inside wizards,
and jinx and Houdini

the fifth lies in conjure,
in sorcery, trick

it's in your perception,
for it is...

Liz Brownlee

Magic

14

A Royal Riddle?

Kings and queens may cling to power
and the jester's got his call.
But, as you may all discover,
the common one outranks them all.

Anon

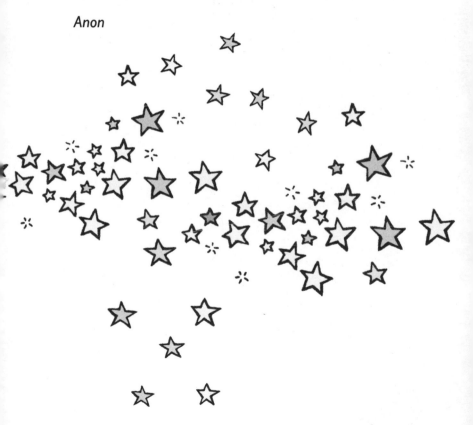

What?

What does man love more than life,
Fear more than death or mortal strife
What the poor have, the rich require
and what contented men desire
What the miser spends and the spendthrift saves
And all men carry to their graves?

Anon

Nothing

Ants

What kind of ants
tear down trees?

What kind of ants
have four knees?

What kind of ants
flap their ears in the breeze?

Shhh! Don't tell —
it's a tease ...

Tony Mitton

Eleph-ants. Elephants really do have four knees, as all four legs
bend forwards (like human knees). In all other quadrupeds only
the front legs bend that way, the back legs bending backwards
(as in horses for example).

17

The Seashore

Tossed into tangles by waves
it drizzles salt-sparkles on to sand.

Soft under seaweed the toe-nipper
waits for new armour.

Pentagram on the beach
fish with a sky-name.

Not for collecting or poking
leave this jelly-mould body for the tide.

In a bowl of barnacled rock a tiny sea
covers sea flowers, shrimps and a crab.

Written in the sand, a seagull's poem
is rubbed out by waves.

As far as the eye can see, scallops
of white embroidery on grey-blue and blue-green.

Holding secret sea-songs and carried home
it spills music into my ear.

Catherine Benson

*Seaweed, a crab, a starfish,
jellyfish, a rock pool, bird prints,
the crests of waves, a shell.*

The Three Rs

I've always been extremely thin
Yet I contain the room I'm in
And I have got the smoothest skin
It's shiny, like a fish's fin
To look at I could be your twin
To find the word that's me just spin
Six letters but you must begin
By making sure there's three Rs in

Nick Toczek

A mirror

19

A Challenging Amount to Digest

I'd like a 7
and an 11.
No better make that 11 a 10
and then
I want a 24.
Actually give me one 24 more
and I'll swap the 10
for another 7 and then
let me see ...
add a 93.
Okay, that'll do.
So what does that come to?

Philip Waddell

*There are two possible
answers to this:
either 155 or around £25
for a Chinese takeaway*

Fingers

They have no flesh, nor feathers,
Nor scales, nor bone
Yet they have fingers and thumbs
Of their own.

Anon

Gloves

Tough Cookies

What Eye Am I?

It's the eye that stares,
The eye that silently follows
The swirl of its coat,
The eye that focuses on
Circling dust particles,
The eye that never squints,
Never blinks, stays steady,
And glides, as its gritty hair
Spins round and round,
It's the eye with tunnel vision.

Coral Rumble

The eye of
a storm

Can You Name These Flowers?

The frozen rain begins to fall,
The frogs shout out before us all,
The country drives in motors, small,
An infant sighs with pleasure.

The sugared pulse is scented bright,
The venomed wyrm can quickly bite,
We look to find what follows night,
Recall me at your leisure.

The cunning creature clothes his hands,
The clotted cream in mugs now stands,
The azure chimes ring o'er the lands,
And we are wed with treasure.

J.H. Rice

*A snowdrop, a crocus (croak before
'us'), a carnation (car-nation), a baby's
breath, a sweet pea, a snapdragon,
a daisy (day-see), a forget-me-not, a
foxglove, a buttercup, a bluebell, a
marigold (marry-gold)*

Lost at Sea

Am I a scarlet alewife
Or a whale of silvery blue?
A fish of brilliant crimson
With fin of vermillion hue?
Peut-être un poisson rouge?
Can you guess which one is true?

Roger Stevens

This is a trick question. I'm a whale
— the others are all red herrings!

Mental Arithmetic

If Mary has three apples
and John has two apples
and Freddie has no apples
and Jenny has an orange
and Simon has two grapefruits
and Ramona has six horses
and Bill has a headache
and Saul has some spinach
and Mo has a new pair of trousers
and Isobel has a liking for hamsters
and Graham has a nose for a bargain
and Crystal has athlete's foot
and Mary still has her three apples
what do *you* have?

A.F. Harrold

This is an even trickier trick question. There's no definite answer, but you must have something!

Three Days in a Row

You can't use Monday
Nor Tuesday, nor Wednesday
Not Thursday, not Friday – okay?
You can't use Saturday in your list
And Sunday also must be missed.
But name me if you think you know
Three days that come all in a row

Anon, put into verse by Jilly Pryor

Yesterday, today and tomorrow

26

A Famous Journey

This riddle is at least 250 years old. There have been many versions of it. The most common was first printed around 1825.

As I was going to St Ives,
I met a man with seven wives,
Each wife had seven sacks,
Each sack had seven cats,
Each cat had seven kits:
Kits, cats, sacks, wives,
How many were going to St Ives?

Because the narrator 'met' the man and his wives, we can assume they are coming from St Ives. In other words he was going to St Ives and they were going in the other direction. So the answer is One, the narrator. The purpose of the riddle is to trick the listener into making long calculations only to be surprised by the simplicity of the answer. If you want to do the sum anyway, you need to add up: 1 man, 7 wives, 49 sacks, 343 cats and 2401 kits, plus the narrator, which equals 2802.

Here's a modern riddle that uses a similar format.

Brothers

As I was on my way to school,
I couldn't help but feel a fool,
I met two brothers much alike
One called Rick and one called Mike.
They shared a face, they shared a name,
The more I looked, I saw the same:
Same hair, same eyes, same grin of mirth,
Same height and weight, same date of birth.
And this is where my quiz begins –
I know for sure they are not twins!

J.H. Rice

I'm sure you've heard of triplets, three:
They are my kin – the third is me!

Keeping with Tradition

In this type of traditional riddle we are given clues to the answer by being told where certain letters are, or are not. For example if 'my first is in cat, but not in bat' then the first letter must be a C. I've included poems that offer a few modern twists on this idea that all centre on finding letters or words.

What Am I?

My first is twice in apple but not once in tart.
My second is in liver but not in heart.
My third is in giant and also in ghost.
Whole I'm best when I am roast.
What am I?

Anon

A pig (with apologies to any vegetarians)

Can You Guess?

Every dawn begins with me
At dusk I'll be the first you see
And daybreak couldn't come without
What midday centre's all about
Daises grow from me, I'm told
And when I come, I end all cold
But in the sun I won't be found
Yet still, each day I'll be around.

Anon

The letter D

And I'll be With You Soon

My first is in head and in program
My second in hands and in neck
My third is in diodes and data
My fourth is in RAM (I'm hi-tech)
My fifth is in cogs and in motors
My sixth in electronic brain
My last is in drivers and digits…
That's all I should need to explain.

Philip Waddell

Android

On Missing L tt r

Try r ading this po m,
I b t you can s ,
my crummy comput r
has on brok n k y.
I'm so disappoint d
I f l lik a j rk,
I pr ss and I push
but that l tt r won't work.
I want d this po m
to b som thing fin ,
with b autiful imag s
lin aft r lin .
But though I hav struggl d
from dusk until dawn,
it's hard to writ w ll
wh n th r 's on l tt r gon .

Eric Ode

The letter e

32

On the Whole

If you're fit and healthy
The answer's in your brains
For if you take the whole away
There's always some remains

Jilly Pryor

Wholesome

Alphabet What?

Throw in two t's
An s
And a g,
Add h and a,
Season with p,
Mix in an i,
Then finally e.
Stir them well,
Unscramble them please,
Pop on a plate
And sprinkle with cheese.

Tracey Blance

Spaghetti

Poetic Styles

All the puzzles in this section follow the rules for different types of poem, for example haiku, tanka and cinquain. As you will see, some poems, such as kennings and acrostics, lend themselves easily to becoming puzzles and can be found as such in writings going back hundreds of years.

Haiku

Under the pillow
part of a six-year-old smile
left for the fairies

Celia Warren

A tooth

Spot the Fairy Tales
or Four Little Haikus

What a grumpy titch.
Won't let us over his bridge!
That grass looks *de-lish*...

Enter if you dare –
three breakfasts; one broken chair.
Off to bed? Beware!

Oh, *Fe Fi Fo Fum!*
What has that lad done to so
annoy his old mum?

Since that witch's spell
he's felt Beastly, none too well.
Hey, who rings that *Belle?*

James Carter

The Three Billy Goats Gruff; Goldilocks and the Three Bears; Jack and the Beanstalk; Beauty and the Beast

What?

Stop!
Name him quietly,
Avoid all movement, as you stand
Kidnapped by his stare,
Envenomed with fear.

Coral Rumble

A snake

What Kind of Poem Is This?

Annoyed, irritated, vexed at being

Cut from the branch
Ripped from the bough
Or torn from the tree
Seething at the hand that
Scoops it from the ground

Stacks it in a bundle
Takes it home
If it could it would bark in fury, for it knows it's been
Collected to be fuel,
Kindling for the fire; and angrily it awaits its fate.

John Dougherty

A cross stick (Acrostic)

How Do You Feel?

the only girl in detention
when there is no one at home
            the only boy at the party
        a game of patience
    sad songs
                    one starling, circling
    just me and my games console
when your face doesn't fit

Roger Stevens

Lonesome

Rebus Poem

👁 'd like 2 B a foot ⚽ er,

but 👁 have ꓕƎƎꓞ ꓕƎƎꓞ

👁 'd like 2 B a 🪨 ★

but 👁 't k b̸ 🐝 p 2 a 🐝 t.

👁 'd like 2 B an astro 0

but 👁 don't like 2 fl 👁

👁 'd like 2 B a TV chef

but ☀ ions make me cr 👁 .

👁 'd like 2 B a detect 🐝

but 👁 haven't got a c 🚽

so 👁 'll wr 👁 te some poe 🌳

and 🪝 ROUND with U.

Jane Clarke

A rebus poem uses pictures for words.

Double Delight!

A thunderstorm struck
though I'd wanted to play
outside in the garden.
But then came a ray
of beautiful sunlight.
The storm had passed by!
Then wow! I saw two of them
crossing the sky.

Robert Schechter

A double rainbow

Conundrum Fun

These are regular puzzles, compiled in the form of poems and rhymes.

Chasing the Answer

Round the rugged rock
The ragged rascal ran
How many Rs are there in that?
Answer me if you can.

Anon

There are no Rs in the word 'that'.

A Noisy Gathering

You'll find us in a parliament
In our hundreds, high above
Or on the corners of the battlefield
As we await our moves

Roger Stevens

A rook – the collective noun for rooks is a parliament; the rook is also a chess piece, sometimes called a castle.

Goo Goo Be Joo – Who?

To see this beast
hook those two
enormous tusks
up on to the ice,
haul its hulking
bulk free from the
frigid waters,
then crawl
away on all fours
like some awkward,
oceanic slug,
who would guess
this clumsy,
cumbersome
creature
could ever be the same
graceful swimmer
or fearsome
'Whale-horse'
the Vikings
so revered?

Graham Denton

What Am I?

Pride comes after a fall.
Loser ahead of winner.
Million before thousand,
And hunger after dinner.

Drenched before the storm.
Soaking after drying.
Afternoon before morning,
And tears come after crying.

A baby appears before birth,
And stars come after night.
Sheep proceed the shepherd,
And a candle before light.

This seems to make no sense,
But soon all will be clear.
Life is full of meanings,
You may find some here.

Doda Smith

A dictionary

46

I Am a Jigsaw

My skin is a puzzle
even to me.
It stretches to reach
the top leaves
on the tree.

You can't move the pieces
although they all fit
quite loosely
but that doesn't matter
a bit.

The jigsaw I'm wearing
is orangey-brown,
the smallest pieces
are furthest
down.

My mum thinks I'm handsome
and so does my Nanna.
We live
together
in the savannah.

Jill Townsend

A giraffe

Two by Two

How good is your knowledge of animals? See if you can identify the creatures described in the couplets. Among the more usual suspects watch out for a few rarer specimens that you might want to look up later.

This creature's amongst the oddest of things
It's poisonous, orange and black, and it sings!

The only mammal with two pairs of knees
And one that I met understood Nepalese!

This gives birth to kittens – ah something you knew!
Well how about this then – it eats its own poo!

This bizarre creature, which tastes with its feet,
Throws up on its dinner before it can eat!

This hasn't a smile... such a shame and a sin,
With forty-four teeth it could have such a grin!

This tastes quite like chicken (in Texas it's said)
And bites, for a while, even after it's dead!

These start out as boys but end up as girls!
The cultured ones often enjoy wearing pearls.

This cannot taste sweet with the tongue in its jaws
And what nightmare creature has eighteen sharp
claws?

Don't be misled... she is not saying grace
Before eating hubby... how horrid and base!

Its feathery feet make its flight very quiet
When hunting the skunk which is part of its diet.

Philip Waddell

A hooded pitohui, an elephant, a rabbit, a
fly, a pig, a rattlesnake, an oyster, a cat,
a praying mantis, a great horned owl

49

Beastly Rhymes

All the answers are animals, with daft rhyming adjectives. The first one's a murky turkey. Now, you try to guess the rest...

I'm a dull Christmas bird
A redbreast who's sad
I'm an overfed feline
A rodent who's mad

I'm an unsteady ass
A bird who's not fast
I'm the only mouse cousin
A flat fish who's last

I'm an ape that's exciting
A croaky equine
I'm a hopper with flu
A sheep waiting in line

I'm a tidier big cat
A very large sow
I'm an unreal reptile
A silly young cow

Jilly Pryor

A neater cheetah, big pig, fake snake, daft calf
A thriller gorilla, hoarse horse, groggy froggy, ewe in a queue
A wonky donkey, slow crow, sole vole, late skate
A murky turkey, sobbin' robin, fat cat, batty ratty

In the Twilight Hours

Early morning,
day dawns.
Cats stretch
and dogs yawn.
The sun smiles
as people rise up out of bed
But I,
I lose my head.

Come the night,
a fading light
gives way to dark.
The skies trade sun
for moon and stars
as people climb the stairs to bed.
And I
regain my head.

Shauna Darling Robertson

A pillow

52

Better

I'm PRETTIER than a princess
STRONGER than a gorilla
CLEVERER than a professor
CUTER than a kitten
FASTER than a torpedo
RICHER than a sultan
FUNNIER than a clown, and
SWEETER than an ice cream.

What am I?

Joshua Seigal

A liar

Playing with Words

It's what most writers enjoy doing, and poets, in particular, love to play with words. It's fun to miss out the rhyming word of a couplet, scramble a word's letters to make an anagram, change the order of lines in a poem or even confuse you with strange punctuation (which, coincidently, also shows us all how important punctuation is). Enjoy the playfulness of these!

A Roman Puzzle

Caesar entered on his head
his helmet on his feet
his sandals in his hand
his sword in his eye
an angry glare.

Anon

*Try adding a comma after the second word of each line.
Does it make sense now?*

After School

emoh emit
pih pih yarooh!
teg gab
tops dad
teg sekib
ladep ladep ladep
pots ta krap
yalp yalp yalp
og emoh
doof
yrots
deb

Hannah Whitley

*Try reading each word backwards.
Is that better?*

Strange Times

Three eights are twenty
four nines are thirty
six eights are forty
eight sevens are fifty
six elevens are sixty
six twelves are seventy
two fives are ten.

Trevor Parsons

*Borrow the first word of line two and put it at the end of line one.
Then repeat it as the first word of line two. Do this with every line. If
you know your times tables you'll easily work this out: three eights are
twenty-four; four nines are thirty-six; six eights are forty-eight...*

Here are two anagram puzzles. Unscramble the words for the answers.

Heart

If you stood upon the moon
What would you see?
Rearrange my heart
It's what you mean to me

Roger Stevens

The Earth

In Other Words...

It's *rare* to be behind
Fleas that are fake
A *bear* that's undressed
Or to fish for a *stake*

Take a *marble* for a wander
Ride this on the *shore*
Put your *pet* in the car
There's a prize in the drawer

I hear sheep on the *table*
The bell sounded for *Gran*
Try paste for a hanging
Or *cart* veg if you can

Take a *liar* by train
Wear a dress, be a *bore*
Cast rain on the flowers
This thorn makes you *sore*

Jilly Pryor

Rear, false, bare, skate, ramble, horse, carpet, reward, bleat, rang,
tapestry, carrot, rail, robe, carnations, rose

58

One Way or Another

When Hannah visited
Dr Awkward
She was quite unprepared
To discover they both
Had something they shared

Roger Stevens

'Hannah' and 'Dr Awkward' are both palindromes – they read the same backwards as forwards.

More or Less

I know a word of letters three.
Add two, and fewer there will be.

Anon

The word 'few.'

Pairs

The first one has a father,
the other's in the sky.

These sell things more cheaply
and these make boats glide by.

This one is a step
and the other is a look.

One is at a dog's end
and one is in a book.

One grows on a fruit tree
until it's ripe with juice,

the other's like this puzzle:
it always comes in twos.

Jill Townsend

Take the first letter of the first line, the second letter of the second line and so on to name this famous structure. Can you see why it's called a Staircase Poem, a form which I believe was devised by the poet John Foster?

Landmark

Little children playing sing
Now, as then, about this thing
Linking two halves of a town...
A lady's told it's falling down.
It's not known when the first was built
To span the waters, stilt to stilt,
I guess because, from shore to shore,
To row across was such a chore.
One stood, in stone, six hundred years,
So talented its engineers,
That gracing now the site we see
Has been in use since Seventy-Three.

Philip Waddell

London Bridge. The London Bridge that was built in 1831 didn't fall
down, but because of increased heavy traffic, by the 1960s it was
beginning to sink. It was bought by an American who shipped it to the
Arizona desert, where it is today. Robert P. McCulloch purchased the
bridge for nearly two and a half million dollars in 1968. McCulloch
has always denied the rumour that he thought he was buying the
much more impressive Tower Bridge. The bridge's predecessor had
crossed the Thames there since the twelfth century but there had
been bridges there, linking the City of London with the south side
of the Thames, since the first was built by the Romans. The London
Bridge that exists today was opened in 1973.

A Shy Poem

You'll find me in a pear, lying on a plate
And in the morning if you get up early
In a tea cup, Earl Grey?
Where the bees sup, early May
Or in an oyster, if you're very, very lucky

Roger Stevens

A pearl

Metaphoricals

These poems use similes, metaphors or other literary tricks to confuse and bamboozle you. In the first, for example, there are no actual marble halls, no fountain, nor a golden apple, but those words aptly describe something else. These are very tricky riddles to solve. See how you get on.

Tasty

In marble halls as white as milk
Lined with a skin as soft as silk
Within a fountain crystal-clear
A golden apple doth appear
No doors there are to this stronghold
Yet thieves break in and steal the gold

Anon

An egg

Orb

At harvest, I'm a pumpkin
A burning, bloodshot cyclop's eye
Sometimes I am a football
A giant has kicked way up high
A watermelon's ghostly grin
A smile lopsided in the sky
Or a single fingernail of God's
But tell me – what am I?

Paul Cookson

Progress

We are soldiers hard and grey
Striding over the land
We are giant, scary skeletons
Humming songs and holding hands
What we carry can't be seen
Though you use it every day
Birds find us very useful
But kites? Please stay away

Roger Stevens

Pylons

I Saw A Bride

I saw a bride splendid in white garments
I saw a woman with children.
The children plump and firm within her arms
But some fell down or strangers took and ate them,
Cut them, sliced them, bit them, baked them, boiled
    them –
Alas, alas, a widow frail and naked
stood by my window in the heavy snow
Imagining, under the white snow, she was a bride
    again.
In time, she sighed, in time.

George Szirtes

An apple tree

A Mixed Bag

I hope you've enjoyed puzzling your way through these poems. Now, can you put everything you've learned into practice? Try solving these final riddles.

Hey, How Did You Get Through Customs with That?

I went on a tropical holiday.
I played in the sea and the sand.
I lay in the shade of the coconut trees
then I carried one home in each hand.

Shauna Darling Robertson

Palm

Three

I am a word of meanings three.
Three ways of spelling me there be.
The first is an odour, a smell if you will.
The second some money, but not in a bill.
The third is past tense, a method of passing things on
    or around.
Can you tell me now, what these words are, that have
    the same sound?

Anon

Scent, cent, sent

Who Needs One?

Yours doesn't need one,
Nor does hers or his.
Its only needs one
When it's trying to say it is.

Annie Fisher

An apostrophe

What Am I?

I shine like a diamond.
I'm raining cats and dogs.
I'm not doing this for my benefit.
I am as soft as a feather,
as fierce as a lion,
as fast as a cheetah
and as quiet as a mouse.
I am more than meets the eye.
I'm always the bridesmaid,
never the bride.
I am like a kid in a candy store.
Avoid me like the plague.

Joshua Seigal

A cliché

What's My Name?

Is it Derek, Garth, Gary
Ruth, Esta or Ellie?
Abdul, Ronald, Rory
Robert, Arthur or Ali?
Edwina, Rita, Ronnie
Gazza, Dan or Donny?

Roger Stevens

No . . . it's Gerard.

Kin to a Cat?

I show up in springtime,
soft, grey and fat.
Don't let my name fool you.
I'm nobody's cat.

You may want to pet me
because of my fur,
but though I feel fluffy,
you won't hear me purr.

B.J. Lee

Pussy willow — a type of catkin. Round, furry and grey, catkins are the spring flowers of the willow tree. The catkins we sometimes know as lambs' tails are the flowers of the hazel tree.

Biblical Character

Five hundred begins it, five hundred ends it,
Five in the middle is seen;
First of all figures, the first of all letters,
Take up their stations between.
Join all together, and then you will bring
Before you the name of an eminent king.

Anon

DAVID (*written in Roman numerals: D=500, V=5, I is the first
number, A is the first letter*)

Mix-up at the Zoo

I've had a mix-up at the zoo.
I don't know what I'm going to do.
Can you see what's going on?
Can you work out what's gone wrong?

The little fish swim to and fro...
And shake their manes of shaggy hair.
The lions give a regal stare,
And trumpet as they plod along.
The elephants are big and strong,
And flutter by on rainbow wings.
The butterflies are fragile things,
And squeeze the breath out of their prey.
The pythons like to laze all day,
And leap about from place to place.
The monkeys like to screech and chase,
And, each year, lay a single egg.

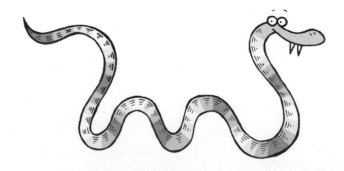

Flamingos stand on one slim leg,
And snap their super-powered jaws.
The crocodiles have powerful claws,
And snuggle in their fluffy coats.
Alpacas live with sheep and goats,
And dive for fish, with snapping beaks.
The penguins give excited squeaks,
Trailing bright bubbles as they go…

Julia Rawlinson

(Look carefully and if you're stuck,
Try reading from the bottom up!)

Run Aground?

I am a boat
That never leaves land
My head's out at sea
But my feet are in sand
I'll steal all your coins
But please don't feel low
For I'll then entertain
With an old-fashioned show

Roger Stevens

A pier

Change of Direction

yrteoP si a drib
tI swonk on reitnorf
fI uoy
kooL, hctaw, netsil
dnA raeh
noitaripsnI si erehwyreve
nI yreve tnemevom
yreve erats
rehtaG sdrow
nipS meht dnuora
daer meht duola
raeH woh yeht dnuos
etirW morf eht traeh
etirW ruoy yaw
uoY yam eb a deshilbup
teoP eno yad

Debra Bertulis

Each word is written backwards, 'Poetry is a bird...'

The Case of the Missing Yorkie

Millie was born on a Monday.
Her favourite pet was a snake.
Her brother, Rob, born on a Friday,
Thought her pet snake a mistake.
Wednesday-born Wendy, their mother,
Agreed Millie's snake was alarming.
But Rollo, the father, born Sunday,
Found the snake placid and charming.

(What is Rollo's son's name?)

The family once had a pet Yorkie.
Her birthday, a Tuesday last May.
Millie's snake hatched four nights later;
It's not hard to figure the day.

(Care to guess?)

The only detective on duty
Examined the evidence while
Millie retired to her bedroom.
Her snake wore a satisfied smile.

(Where did the pup go?)

Steven Withrow

Rob, Saturday, into the snake

A Cunning Plan

In ancient times there was a man
Who came up with a cunning plan
He claimed that he would show to all
The way to see right through a wall
It wasn't magic, nor X-ray
But places still use it today

Anon, put into verse by Jilly Pryor

A window

Funny

I can be cracked
I can be made
I can be told
I can be played
What am I?

Anon

A joke

It's Black and White

My words are always angry
I am often in the news
There's only one answer
Yet many, many clues

Sue Hardy-Dawson

A crossword puzzle

PART TWO
HOW TO WRITE
PUZZLE POEMS

This section of the book is written for all you talented young readers who fancy having a go at writing some puzzling rhymes.

If you've read my book, *Is This a Poem?* you'll know that puzzle poems and riddles sit on the edge of what is and isn't poetry. Some people say they are not, strictly speaking, poems. While other people argue that because these kinds of riddles and rhymes go back a long way and have been written and spoken by some of the very best poets, they do qualify.

Riddlers have included Ancient Greeks, such as Lycophron, who riddled for the Egyptian king Ptolemy, and the famous mathematician Archimedes. And even though the great philosopher Aristotle didn't write puzzle poems himself, he collected riddles written by others. Lots of wordplay, including the palindrome, dates back to Roman times, and in the early seventeenth century the playwright Shakespeare loved puns and word puzzles. In more modern times, J.R.R. Tolkein famously included lots of riddles in *The Hobbit* and *The Lord of the Rings*.

As always, when writing, you must remember that practice, as they say, makes perfect. Your first few attempts may not be very good, but the more you do it the better you will become. Write your poems in rough (as a first draft) and don't be afraid to change them, cross bits out and add new bits, until you have the best you can possibly do. And always read your work out loud. That way you'll get a better feel for the rhythm of the poem. So good luck, and here we go...

A Simple Riddle

Think of an object. Anything you like – something you can see as you look around the room, or something you bought in a supermarket, or something you found in a forest, or an object you collected at the seaside.

I'm going to choose my mug. It's right here by my laptop. First of all, I will write down as many things as I can about my mug. Then I want you to do the same with your object. Here are some questions you could ask yourself:

> *How big is it?*
> *Does its shape remind me of anything?*
> *What is it made of?*
> *What is it used for?*
> *Is it decorative?*
> *Does it have markings?*
> *Is it rough or smooth?*
> *What colour is it?*
> *Does it have any memories for me?*
> *How do I feel about it?*
> *Do I have any other information about it?*
> *Does the word itself have any other meanings?*

Write everything quickly, without too much thought. Then read what you have written and see if the words and phrases give you any new ideas.

This is what I've written about my mug:

It's roughly the size of my hand.
It has a handle.
It's made of china.
It holds drinks. Especially tea, coffee or hot chocolate.
It has the letters S-A-M on it.
It is very smooth and shiny white.
The words are in pink and yellow.
I bought it in the USA, at Seattle Art Museum.
I like it.
A mug is someone who is taken for a fool.
A mug is also slang for someone's face.
To mug up on something is to revise.

Now I am going to choose some phrases for my poem. They mustn't be too obscure – no one is going to know that I bought it at an art gallery, for example. On the other hand you don't want to make it too obvious. Let's see...

It's the size of my hand.
It's made of smooth white china. (I've just picked it up, to feel it. And it's cold, because it's empty. When it's full it's hot. I can maybe use that in my poem.)
It has hot chocolate in it.
(Maybe I can think of a simile for that. What else is hard and solid but inside contains something hot, sweet and delicious? Now I've just remembered the wonderful feeling of drinking a hot drink outdoors, when it's cold, on bonfire night for example.)

I'm nobody's fool. (So I'm not a mug.)

I'm now going to write the draft of the poem. I'm not going to use the word 'mug' at all, because that will be the answer to the puzzle. I've decided to write in the first person, in other words using 'I am...'

Once I've chosen the lines I might use, I need to put them in order. For a puzzle poem, it is usually best to start with the most difficult clue and make them easier as the poem progresses. You don't want to give away the answer too soon.

I'll start like this:

I am the size of a man's hand.
Feel my hard, shiny surface.
When I am empty I am cold.
When I am full, my hot, sweet liquid
Can keep you warm and happy on cold, frosty nights.
I'm nobody's fool.
So what am I?

Nearly there. This poem doesn't have to rhyme. But I've spotted a little alliteration I might add. And also a better way to join up the first two lines. Finally I'll read the poem out loud to make sure it has a nice flow.

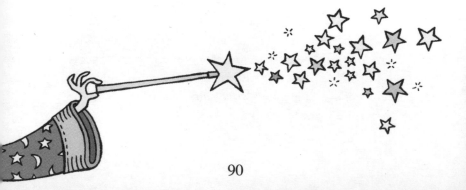

Here's the final poem:

I am the size of the hands
that clasp me tightly
When I'm empty, I'm cold
but now I am full, and hot
and my sweet contents
will bring you contentment
beneath the stars.
I'm nobody's fool.
Or maybe I am?

If you read that as a puzzle poem, would you guess the answer was 'a mug'?

How have you got on compiling your list about your object? Are you happy with your final puzzle poem? Keep working on it, till you feel it's right. Then try it out on your family or friends and see if they can guess what you were thinking about.

Kennings

A kenning describes something familiar in an uncommon way, without using its name. Kennings were first used in Anglo-Saxon and Norse poetry. The famous Anglo-Saxon poem *Beowulf* uses many kennings, for example the body is a 'bone house', the term 'whale-road' is used for the sea, 'battle sweat' is used for blood and a ship is a 'wave floater'.

Kennings are sometimes metaphorical. For example, looking at the kennings above, the body is not really a house, but it does provide a house for our bones; the sea is not really a road but it is the thing that whales travel in, so it acts like a road for them.

Kennings were not originally written as guessing games, but as the descriptive language in poems and stories. But because the real name of the subject is not given, they make great puzzles. Especially when put together in a list.

Now shall we go about writing one? First of all, let's think of a subject. Something fairly well known, but not too obvious. It can be a thing. Or an animal. Or a person. As I write this, I'm thinking about the football team I support (Liverpool!). So I'm going to choose something to do with football players. How about the goalkeeper?

I'm going to think of as many words and phrases connected with a goalkeeper that I can. For example: *He or she stands in the goal. Stops the ball. Catches the ball. Punches it away. They dive. They're brave. They jump.*

They roll. They have quick reflexes. They're a defender. Wear a different colour jumper. Have nothing to do a lot of the time. Throw the ball out. Take goal kicks. Help make the wall. Shout at the team. Organise the defence. Save penalties.

You could do this by writing the word down in the middle of the page and making a spider diagram. Now try and turn some of these into two-word phrases.

I have made:

Ball stopper
Ball catcher
Ball puncher
Fast diver
Safe catcher
Penalty saver
Crowd pleaser
Wall builder
Game winner
Team organiser
Hoarse shouter
Muddy scrambler
Long kicker
Game sorter
Brave diver
Stand arounder
Ace defender

That would make a good kenning and I'm quite pleased with it. But I want to improve it. Some of the word pairs are better than others. Is *'arounder'* actually a word? I don't think it is! 'Fast diver' and 'brave diver' are a bit too similar. I'll cross out the pairs that I think are weak. I also don't want to make the answer too obvious, so I'll leave out references to the ball. I'll change the order too. I think it should end with 'game winner' don't you? And it's too long. Here's my final attempt:

Wall builder
Hoarse shouter
Smart mover
Quick responder
Team sorter
Long kicker
Brave diver
Deft handler
Lightning stopper
Top defender
Game winner

Ready-made Puzzle Poems

I am NOT suggesting that you copy or steal from other poets or writers. What I AM suggesting is that you take a well known riddle and turn it into a short puzzle poem. There are a lot of anonymous and traditional Christmas-cracker-type riddles and poems that you can use for inspiration, or you could find a simple rhyme and write it down in a straightforward way. For example: *When is a door not a door? When it's a jar.*

In this poem, I thought of the last line first, and then searched for a word to rhyme with it. So there is *jam...* and *am.*

> When I'm open or closed I'm a door
> It's obvious that's what I am
> But when I'm neither open or closed
> I'm a place to put your jam

The following examples play around with one of the oldest jokes there is – *Why did the chicken cross the road?* Find a joke book and have some fun!

Did the egg come first? Or was it me?
Even scholars can't agree.
But every person you might meet
Knows just why I crossed the street
What am I?

Or

Why did the chicken cross the road?
To get to the other side.
But why did the chicken cross the playground?
To get to the other slide.

The Traditional Riddle

My first is in rhyme but isn't in time
My second's in mint but isn't in thyme
My third is in add but not in take away
My fourth's in divide but not multiply
My fifth starts lackadaisically
My sixth ends with resolve
My whole is a puzzle that you have to solve

Riddles that play around with letters may appear tricky to write, and the following explanation is a bit complicated – but bear with me. Once you get the hang of things you'll find it's really not that hard. And it's lots of fun!

In the first line of the above example, 'My first is in rhyme...' means that the first letter of the answer is R, H, Y, M or E. '... but isn't in time'. And we are told that it isn't a T, I, M or E. So it has to be R, H or Y.

Similarly in line two we can work out that the second letter of the word must be an I or an N.

The letter in line three can only be a D.

Line four is a D, V or E.

Line five tells us that the next letter is L. (It starts the word *lackadaisically*.)

Line six suggests the sixth letter is at the end of resolve. (So it's an E.)

And the last line gives a clue to the meaning of the word. Looking at the possible letter clues from the first six lines, we can deduce it is a RIDDLE!

Let's have a go at writing our own. First choose the subject of your riddle. Choose something that your readers will be familiar with. But not something too obvious. There are already lots of riddles about clocks, time, rivers and chairs and tables. Animals make a good subject – but try to go for less obvious ones. Pick a word that's not too long, I would say a maximum of eight letters. For now, let's use RHINO.

Just like in the poem above, we are going to hint at each letter of the word RHINO. But we're going to do more than just find words that contain the right letters to spell out our answer. We're looking for rhymes – and a poem that makes sense.

For our first line, we need a word that has an R in it, and a second word that contains no R. Not any old words – they need to be related in some way. And if they link to a rhino, that's good too. A rhino likes to visit watering holes. So how about water and mud. There's an R in water but not one in mud.

I'm going to use capital letters here to show where our clues are, but they won't be in the final poem. We can write:

My first is in wateR but isn't in mud.

Now on to the second line. We need a word to rhyme with 'mud' that has no H. Blood? Flood? Let's choose flood. Now we need a word that does contain an H that is connected to the word flood. Think about weather. Sunshine? So we have:

My first is in wateR but isn't in mud

My second's in sunsHine but isn't in flood

Let's do the same for the next two lines. We are looking at the letters I and N. And we're sticking to the subject. Rhinos are pretty big and they run and charge.

My third is in massIve but isn't in large

My fourth is in runNing but isn't in charge

Now we have to help the reader find the final letter. And give a clue to the whole word. We also need to make the last two lines rhyme.

A tip is to start with the final line because it's often easier to find a rhyme if you work backwards from the end of a poem.

Think about a rhino – it's a bit like a tank, isn't it, and it can be quite dangerous. So how about:

My whole's like a tank – best keep out of my way.

We can perhaps improve on that later. Notice that I've chosen a last word that is easy to rhyme with – there are lots of words that rhyme with the sound 'ay'.

So, working backwards, we need a line that hints at the last letter of RHINO. An O actually looks like a zero as well, doesn't it. And zero means nothing. So I'm thinking:

My fifth shows that I have nOthing to say.

And here's our finished riddle:

My first is in water but isn't in mud
My second's in sunshine but isn't in flood
My third is in massive but isn't in large
My fourth is in running but isn't in charge
My fifth shows that I have nothing to say
My whole's armour-plated – best keep out of my way.

I hope that you will now want to make up your own riddles and have a go at writing some puzzle poems. And when you've written a poem, it would be great if you could send it to me at The Poetry Zone (you can find details at the beginning of the book). You could also make your own book of puzzle poems and riddling rhymes. Everyone loves a riddle – one Christmas we made our own crackers and made up our own riddles to put in them. But whatever you decide to do, I'm sure you will have fun!

Acknowledgements

'The Seashore' © Catherine Benson. Published in The Universal Vacuum Cleaner and Other Riddle Poems, ed. John Foster (Oxford University Press, 2005), A Million Brilliant Poems (Part One): A collection of the very best children's poetry today, ed. Roger Stevens (A & C Black Childrens & Educational, 2010), First Comprehension Book 2 by Celia Warren (Schofield & Sims Ltd, 2014) and The Works 6: Assembly Poems, ed. Pie Corbett (Macmillan Children's Books, 2007); 'Change of Direction' © Debra Bertulis; 'Alphabet What?' and 'An Unusual Pet' © Tracey Blance 2018, reprinted by permission of the author; 'Find Me' © Liz Brownlee; 'Spot the Fairy Tales' © James Carter; 'Rebus Poem' © Jane Clarke; 'Orb' © Paul Cookson; 'Hey, How Did You Get Through Customs with That?' and 'In the Twilight Hours' © Shauna Darling Robertson; 'Goo Goo Be Joo – Who?' © Graham Denton; 'What Kind of Poem Is This?' © John Dougherty; 'A Place to Puzzle' and 'Who Needs One?' © Annie Fisher; 'It's Black and White' © Sue Hardy-Dawson; 'Mental Arithmetic' © A. F. Harrold, reproduced by kind permission of the author; 'Kin to a Cat?' © B. J. Lee; 'Under the Bridge' © Suzy Levinson; 'Ants' © Tony Mitton. Published in A Trunkful of Elephants, ed. Judith Nicholls (Methuen Children's Books, 1994); 'Second-Hand Poem' © Laura Mucha; 'On Missing L tt r' © Eric Ode; 'Strange Times' © Trevor Parsons; 'A Cunning Plan', 'Beastly Rhymes', 'In Other Words...', 'On the Whole', 'Three Days in a Row' © Jilly Pryor; 'Mix-up at the Zoo' © Julia Rawlinson; 'Brothers' and 'Can You Name These Flowers' © J. H. Rice; 'What' and 'What Eye Am I?' © Coral Rumble;

'Splash!' © Carol Samuelson-Woodson; 'Double Delight!' © Robert Schechter; 'Better' and 'What Am I?' © Joshua Seigal; 'What Am I?' © Doda Smith; 'I Saw A Bride' © George Szirtes; 'The Three Rs' © Nick Toczek; 'I Am a Jigsaw' and 'Pairs' © Jill Townsend 2019; 'A Challenging Amount to Digest', 'And I'll be With You Soon', 'Two by Two' and 'Landmark' © Philip Waddell; 'Haiku' © Celia Warren 2019; 'After School' © Hannah Whitley; 'The Case of the Missing Yorkie' © Steven Withrow 2018.

All efforts have been made to seek permission for copyright material, but in the event of any omissions, the publisher would be pleased to hear from the copyright holders and to amend these acknowledgements in in subsequent editions.

More Poetry from
Roger Stevens

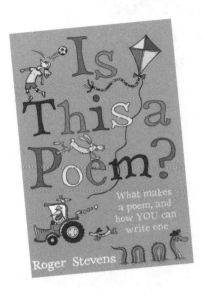

Whether you want poems to learn by heart or are wondering what on earth a poem is anyway, look out for more poetry anthologies from Roger Stevens and Bloomsbury Education.

Is this a Poem
9781472920010

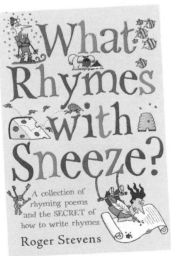

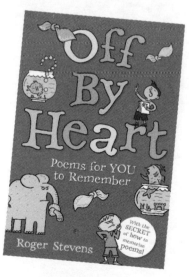

Off By Heart
9781408192948

What Rhymes with Sneeze
9781408155769

FOR **MORE** FROM SOME OF THE **BRILLIANT POETS** FEATURED IN THIS BOOK VISIT WWW.BLOOMSBURY.COM

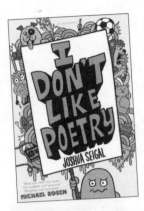

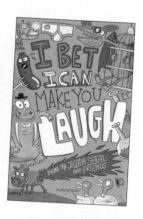

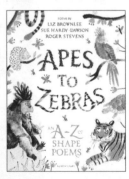